ONE-MINUTE
PRAYERS®

for

Graduates

HARVEST HOUSE PUBLISHERS
EUGENE, OREGON

Cover by Bryce Williamson

ONE-MINUTE PRAYERS is a registered trademark of The Hawkins Children's LLC. Harvest House Publishers, Inc., is the exclusive licensee of the federally registered trademark ONE-MINUTE PRAYERS.

ONE-MINUTE PRAYERS® FOR GRADUATES

Published by Harvest House Publishers
Eugene, Oregon 97408
www.harvesthousepublishers.com

ISBN 978-0-7369-1285-3
ISBN 978-0-7369-7276-5 (eBook)

Printed in China

18 19 20 21 22 23 24 25 26 / RDS-SK / 10 9 8 7 6 5 4 3 2 1

Contents

A World of
Opportunity

THE NEXT STEPS

Dear God, I am grateful for this chance to turn an important page in my life story. Graduation brings so many opportunities—jobs, internships, military service, or a more advanced degree or certification. As I complete various applications and interact with new people, please calm my heart. May your peace take the place of my insecurities and doubts and raw nerves.

As I take the next steps toward my future, remind me to breathe, to be honest, and to simply be myself. Thank you again for opening the door of opportunity to me. May I walk through the doorway in your strength and grace. Amen.

> Whatever you do, work at it with all your heart,
> as working for the Lord, not for human masters.

COLOSSIANS 3:23

A New Season of Life

Creator God, at the start of this new season of life, please be with me as I gaze into the distance at a world full of possibilities. A world of hopes and dreams, opportunities and challenges.

Please take my fears and turn them into opportunities to grow. Empower me when my faith grows weak. Through all the seasons of my life, please walk with me. Remind me that I am not alone. You will be with me in my victories and my defeats.

> May the Lord our God be with us as he was with our ancestors; may he never leave us nor forsake us. May he turn our hearts to him, to walk in obedience to him.
>
> **1 KINGS 8:57-58**

A License to Learn

Dear all-knowing heavenly Father, I praise and thank you for new opportunities to learn and grow. It's hard to believe, but I'm officially a *graduate*! I can't wait to see what's next in my life!

Please open my eyes and my mind to new truths and insights. Nurture in me a hunger for knowledge. I want my diploma to be more than an acknowledgment of what I have already learned. I want it to be a license for a bright future. I want it to encourage me to learn even more.

As I learn, balance my curiosity with contemplation and prayer. Be with me as I venture into adulthood. May I always build my life from a foundation of truth. Amen.

The humble will see their God at work and be glad.

PSALM 69:32 NLT

PRIORITIES IN PLACE

THE GREATEST GIFT

Lord, thank you for all the gifts you have given me here on earth. I am incredibly fortunate, especially in light of how people my age in other parts of the world have to live.

However, I want to value my spiritual gifts and blessings more than anything in the material world. I don't want to get too attached to any of my "stuff." And I don't want to value anything more than I value you.

Please help me order my priorities—with you always at the top of the list. And if that means giving up something, so be it. I ask for the strength to do the right thing.

I praise you for being the greatest gift of all. Amen.

What good is it for someone to gain the whole
world, and yet lose or forfeit their very self?

LUKE 9:25

Someday or Today?

————

I have so many hopes and dreams right now. So much that I hope will happen…someday. I am full of good intentions. But I know that an intention is not the same thing as a plan, a commitment, or an achievement. May I avoid letting opportunities slip through my fingers.

Help me to set priorities and timelines. Give me the discipline to make a to-do list and start getting things done. I don't have an endless supply of time, even though it might seem that way right now. Time is a gift from you. Guide me so that I will use that gift wisely. Help me to focus less on someday and more on today.

> Don't brashly announce what you're
> going to do tomorrow.
>
> **PROVERBS 27:1 MSG**

First Things First

———

I love it when my life overflows with blessings. But when it overflows with deadlines, responsibilities, and new schedules? Not so much.

There are so many new things in my life, I'm not sure where to put them all. And it seems like not everything is going to fit. So, what do I leave in? What can I leave out? I need your help here.

Help me figure out what is a "must" and what is optional or no longer important. Relationships, rest, work, spirituality, health—I need help with it all. I don't want what is seemingly urgent to crowd out what is truly important. Please be my guide. I want my life to be more than adequate or even good. I want it to be great.

> Seek first his kingdom and his righteousness, and
> all these things will be given to you as well.
>
> **MATTHEW 6:33**

The Master Plan

———

At this point in life, I find myself making all kinds of plans and setting a variety of goals. The possibilities seem endless. Help me craft my plans carefully and prayerfully. Don't let me fall into the trap of making random plans and then asking you to bless them. I don't want you to be an afterthought. I want you to be the ultimate source and inspiration for my plans and goals. I don't want to spend the next few years chasing after the wind.

I commit to planning with care, to seeking wise advice, and to making sure each goal is based on healthy desires and ambitions. I want to make sure my plans are in line with your master plan. I want my ideas, skills, and energy to make this world a better place.

> Be careful that you do not forget the Lord your God, failing to observe his commands, his laws and his decrees that I am giving to you this day.
>
> **DEUTERONOMY 8:11**

Find a Foundation

————

As a recent graduate, I am thankful that I have learned so much. But sometimes I wonder if it's *too* much. In a year, how much of what I have learned will I be able to remember? It's hard to hold on to facts and concepts if I don't apply them in my everyday life. This reminds me of your promise that hearing your Word and putting it into practice is like building a house on a solid-rock foundation.

I want to build my life on you, not my own opinions or emotions. Not on the shifting sands of what's popular. I want to build a life that will withstand the storms that will inevitably come my way. Please help me build that life. Please be my foundation.

> Everyone who hears these words of mine
> and puts them into practice is like a wise
> man who built his house on the rock.
>
> **MATTHEW 7:24**

Each Day Is a Gift

When I talk with friends my own age, I notice that we all seem to think, "We're young…we have all the time in the world." I know this kind of thinking can be dangerous. None of us is guaranteed more than the present moment. Time is like a lot of other things in life—we use it or we lose it.

Help me to make the most of my time *right now*. Help me to set wise priorities. I am (usually) inspired when I remember that time is a great equalizer. We all get the same 24-hour days, from the president to the postal worker to the poorest guy in town. It's not about how much time we possess. It's about how much time we use and how wisely we use it.

I pray that I will see each new day as a gift—a gift I will be grateful for and use for good.

> Make the most of every opportunity
> you have for doing good.
>
> **EPHESIANS 5:16 TLB**

To Defend and Protect

One way you express your kindness, grace, and righteousness is by defending and protecting people—especially those who are most vulnerable in our world. May I never leave a vulnerable, hurting person exposed to harm of any kind. May I always stand up for what is right. May I remember that when I protect, encourage, and help "the least of these," I am helping Jesus himself.

Please give me the courage to stand, even when it feels as if I am standing alone. And thank you for the assurance that I am never actually alone, for you are always with me.

They caused the cry of the poor to come before him, so that he heard the cry of the needy.

JOB 34:28

GIVING PRAISE

The God of Creation

———————

Creator God, I praise you today for the beauty of your earth, from the flowers and trees springing from the ground to the birds soaring in the sky. I don't think that we, your people, are as grateful as we should be for our earthly home, where we can see your greatness, majesty, and mind-blowing creativity.

I pray that I will go outside more and enjoy your presence in the fresh air and open spaces. When I experience your creation, I learn more about you. And I grow more thankful for this world that I get to be a part of.

> I will exalt you, my God the King;
> I will praise your name for ever and ever...
> Great is the Lord and most worthy of praise;
> his greatness no one can fathom.
> One generation commends your works to another;
> they tell of your mighty acts.

PSALM 145:1-4

Moments to Remember

M y life has been filled with beautiful moments I will never forget. I know that these moments are gifts from your hand. I will never forget doing the things I love with the people I love. You send these moments to remind me that your supply of love and kindness will never run dry.

I hope my gratitude won't run out either. Help me keep my eyes, mind, and heart open to receive your blessings, both small and large. Who knows what divine moments are about to unfold, filling my heart with joy? I thank you for the memories made and the memories yet to be created!

> In the morning, Lord, you hear my voice;
> in the morning I lay my requests before you
> and wait expectantly.
>
> **PSALM 5:3**

Divine Empathy

———

I am awestruck when I think about how Jesus, God the Son, could have come to earth as a superhuman hero, or at least a fully mature adult. Instead, he chose to experience every stage of life from infancy to adulthood. This means that you, my Savior, know what it's like to be my age. You endured your share of many of the same struggles I face every day. You are familiar with my every heartache and my every joy.

I thank you for the comforting truth that you understand from experience what it's like to be me. And you always will. I will change with time and age. Your love will not. That amazes me. It humbles me too.

> We proclaim to you what we have seen and heard,
> so that you also may have fellowship with us. And
> our fellowship is with the Father and with his Son,
> Jesus Christ. We write this to make our joy complete.
>
> **1 JOHN 1:3-4**

Unbottled Emotions

I haven't said, "Praise God" or anything like that in too long. It's not that I haven't been thankful or haven't seen your hand at work in my life. But sometimes I don't take the time to truly celebrate your goodness, your kindness, and the flat-out amazing things you do for your people.

Please tear down the barriers encasing my emotions. I want to share those moments of absolute joy with you, the one who makes them happen. I want to show my friends and family what it means to be delighted by my heavenly Father. To put it simply, I need to get over myself and celebrate the goodness that you bring to life. Restore in me the wonder of living life as a child of God. Amen—and praise God!

> The living, the living—they praise you,
> as I am doing today.
>
> **ISAIAH 38:19**

GIVING THANKS

The Gift of Life

Lord, thank you for giving me life. I'm amazed every time I try to wrap my mind around the fact that you know me by name. I'm grateful for being a part of your family. You welcomed me with open arms, and I know my life will never be the same. It's a great privilege to be in your family. It's also an awesome responsibility.

You are my father in heaven. You mean the world to me, and I hope my life will be something that makes you proud. Please keep my eyes focused on you. I want to start each day with the desire to make my life count for something good. *Your* good.

> You have searched me, LORD,
> and you know me.
> You know when I sit and when I rise;
> you perceive my thoughts from afar.

PSALM 139:1-2

A Legacy of Goodness

Dear Father God, thank you for your unfailing love for me. Thank you for your blessings and the goodness of your heart. I praise you for guiding me through so many times of uncertainty and pain. When I was lowest, you rescued me and set me on top of the highest mountain.

I thank you for the Bible, which comforts me when I am depressed. And I love how it reminds me of the faithfulness you have shown to your people over and over and over.

For thousands of years, people have seen true help and hope coming from you. I am grateful to be one of those people.

The Lord will indeed give what is good.

PSALM 85:12

Coming Through

———

Today I find myself basking in the warmth of answered prayers. I am amazed at how you come through for me again and again. And so many times, you answer me in astonishing and unexpected ways. You don't always give me what I want, but you have always given me what I need.

I'm humbled by how faithful you are to your people—to people just like me. You are kind to us collectively and individually. When I come to you with a sincere heart, you provide love and kindness and wisdom that rock my world. For this, and for so many other reasons, I thank you with my whole heart.

> I am convinced that nothing can ever separate
> us from God's love…Nothing in all creation will
> ever be able to separate us from the love of
> God that is revealed in Christ Jesus our Lord.

ROMANS 8:38-39 NLT

Bless Those Who Bless Me

———

I realize I don't thank you enough for my friends, my family, my leaders, and all those who travel through life with me. I am grateful to you for the people who support me, care for me, and show me wisdom. They are not perfect; that's for sure. (Neither am I.) But I need to be honest right now and realize that life would be so much harder, if not impossible, without them.

So with a thankful heart, I ask you to bless the people who have blessed me so much in good times and in hard times. Life is not just about where we are going; it's also about who is traveling with us. Thank you for all my traveling companions!

Instruct the wise and they will be wiser still;
teach the righteous and they will add to their learning.

PROVERBS 9:9

Grateful = Happy

If there is one thing I have learned in my life, it's that grateful people are happy people. A lack of gratitude robs the mind and the soul of joy. Every day that I forget this truth tends to be a very bad day.

Help me to avoid falling into a haze of ingratitude. Don't let me miss the chance to be truly grateful for every small blessing. May I live thankfully. And on those days when I feel too busy or too stressed to pause and thank you? That's when I should thank you even more. That's when I can be sure I am about to miss the joy of living gratefully. There are days when I need to stop over-thinking and over-worrying my life. I need to simply say, "Thank you, Lord." This is one of those days.

True godliness with contentment is itself great wealth.

1 TIMOTHY 6:6 NLT

HOW'S YOUR PERSPECTIVE?

Lost Perspective?

―――――

Sometimes I ask myself how well I truly know you, and I'm troubled by the answer. I don't know you as well as I should. Sometimes I let other things crowd you out of my day, and those days can grow into weeks or even months.

I'm sorry for letting other things become more important than they should be. I need to regain my perspective on life. Help me make time for you. I *need* that time. Then, as I deal with all those other priorities (and non-priorities), make me aware of your presence all the time.

> If anyone serves, they should do it with the
> strength God provides, so that in all things
> God may be praised through Jesus Christ.

1 PETER 4:11

An Attitude of Gratitude?

———

I ask your forgiveness for my ingratitude. No, my life is not perfect, and you know the heartbreak I have already suffered in my young life. But I have so much, and I have to confess that in some ways I have wasted a lot. I have wasted time. I have wasted talent. I have wasted money.

The more I look around, the more I realize how many people lack the basics of life—things like food and shelter and family. So I want to stop and thank you for all you have given me and my family. I pray that my gratitude will grow into generosity.

Please give me compassion for those people who lack the basics. Show me how I can help them in some way.

He will rescue the poor when they cry to him;
he will help the oppressed, who have no one to defend them.
He feels pity for the weak and the needy...
For their lives are precious to him.

PSALM 72:12-14 NLT

THE GIFT OF TODAY

———

Every time I read a news story or social media post about someone who has passed away, I am reminded that we humans are fragile creatures and that life is unpredictable.

I know life can be short, but I trust that my life will be exactly long enough for you to accomplish your purposes in me.

I am young and strong, but I don't know how long my life will be. But I do know that today is an amazing gift from you. Let me treasure each day as an opportunity to make my world a little bit better…in your name. Amen.

The work of God is this: to believe in the one he has sent.

JOHN 6:29

Above the Noise

———

It's a noisy world. I am thankful that your promises rise above the chaos and chatter. Your love stands tall when corporations and governments stumble and fall. When you give your word, you mean business. Thank you for all the tangible reminders of your love and power. The stars you set in space. The rainbows you hang in the sky.

And let me always remember the smaller (but no less important) signs of your love. The lyrics from my favorite song. The hug from that person who understands me best and keeps on loving me in spite of myself. I can find your love in so many places. Even the pages of a book.

I've banked your promises in the vault of my heart.

PSALM 119:11 MSG

Rock Solid

———

Dear God, the Bible calls you the rock. That's a great image for me because I see you as the rock of my life. Solid. Secure. You are always there for me. You can't be pushed around. You are my shelter when the storms of life pour down on me.

And on other days, you are my higher place. You let me see my world with clarity and with rock-solid hope.

So I thank you for being my rock. With you as my foundation, I know I will be able to stand strong.

The Lord is my rock, my protection, my Savior...
I can run to him for safety.

PSALM 18:2 NCV

A Moment of Peace?

Life after graduation means new schedules, new responsibilities. Sometimes it's a struggle to get out the door on time with the things I need to face the day. It's a storm of stress.

Lord, help me to begin each day better. Before I turn my mind to the challenges waiting for me, let me find peace and perspective in you. Give me a humble spirit. Remind me that I am loved and that you have a purpose for me. Ultimately, my life is about serving you, and I know you are on my side. You want me to succeed. You want me to be fulfilled.

So the next time I feel stressed, complaining, "Where are my car keys?" or "Where is my phone charger?" may I ask a more important question: "Where is my heart?"

Show me your ways, LORD, teach me your paths.
Guide me in your truth and teach me.

PSALM 25:4

The Gift of the Struggle

_____

Lord, I thank you for your strength in the times of my greatest needs and darkest fears. Even though I am young, I marvel at how many times you have been with me (and *for* me) during emotional, physical, spiritual, and financial struggles.

Difficult times have helped me understand myself better. More important, they have helped me gain a deeper understanding of your grace and love. I have a better perspective on life than I did even just a year or two ago. I can offer my support and encouragement to others because of the real-life wisdom you have provided me. Thank you for the gift of contentment, even in trying times.

Consider it pure joy, my brothers and sisters, whenever you face trials of many kinds, because you know that the testing of your faith produces perseverance.

JAMES 1:2-3

FRIENDS AND FAMILY

My Circle of Friends

———

Dear God, you are the Lord of all things, and that includes my friendships. I am excited for the chance to meet new people, but I want to choose my friends with thought and care. So I ask you to guard my friendships. Keep me from any relationship that might damage me in the short run or the long run.

I don't want to judge others for thinking or believing differently from me, but I don't want to compromise my values either. Help me to walk this thin line with great care and humility.

May I be a true friend to the people in my circle. I look to you as I hope to expand that circle. Please bring me deep friendships that will stand the test of time.

And thank you for being my best friend! Amen.

There are "friends" who destroy each other,
but a real friend sticks closer than a brother.

PROVERBS 18:24 NLT

The Real Me

———

Today, my thoughts turn to certain people in my life—friends, relatives, friends of friends, and so on—who need to know you. I wish they knew you as well as I do. I pray that they will open their hearts and minds to your love and wisdom. I long for them to see you as you really are.

Help me do my part to share your love, grace, and wisdom with everyone I encounter. I know I am imperfect, but you don't demand perfection of me—just faithfulness and an honest heart. I long for people to encounter the real you. By being the real me, the me you created, perhaps I can help.

Use your freedom to serve one another in love.

GALATIANS 5:13 NLT

A Prayer for My Friends

──────

Mighty God, I ask you to please look after the friends I leave behind as I move forward on this journey. We've been through a lot together, and you have used them to encourage me and to teach me many important lessons about friendship and loyalty.

Help me to remember them in my prayers and to hold on to the value of our friendships. I don't want to forget them in the busy days ahead. Don't let my heart drift away from the people who have come to mean so much to me. I thank you for each one of these special friends.

Please watch over them and protect them from the dangers of this world until we can laugh together once again.

Amen.

Every good and perfect gift is from above,
coming down from the Father of the heavenly lights.

JAMES 1:17

GRATITUDE FOR MY ROCK STARS

God, you know my heart is thankful for so many things. When I really take the time to think about the ways you have blessed me, I am totally amazed!

One of the most obvious blessings right now is the set of amazing people you put in my life to guide me and teach me. There have been so many who cared about me, nurtured me, and set wonderful examples for me.

I thank you for each teacher, coach, relative, or friend who took time to shape and guide my life. I ask your blessing on every one. For all those who have cared about me and simply refused to let me fail, I truly thank you!

I can only hope to be such a blessing to the younger people I encounter in my future.

Thank you, Lord.

Now we ask you, brothers and sisters, to acknowledge those who work hard among you, who care for you in the Lord and who admonish you. Hold them in the highest regard in love because of their work. Live in peace with each other.

1 THESSALONIANS 5:12-13

FORGIVENESS

Sinking Sins

As you know, Lord, I messed up. Big-time. I know I disappointed other people, and I'm disappointed in myself as well. I would give just about anything to go back in time and do things differently. More than anything else, I am sorry I let *you* down.

At times like this, I am comforted by your promise that you forgive all my sins. You sink them to the bottom of the ocean. I love that picture, especially at times like this.

You don't hold my sins against me. And you don't want them to hold me back from being who you want me to be. I struggle to find the words to thank you for this kind of grace.

I praise you and thank you that every sin, including *that* one, is forgiven and forgotten.

You'll sink our sins to the bottom of the ocean.

MICAH 7:19 MSG

Losing Sight

————

I ask your forgiveness because I have lost sight of my goals. What's more, I have lost sight of who I truly am. I'm letting others define me rather than establishing my own identity in you.

Forgive me for losing control. Forgive me for believing lies about myself and forgetting your truth. I know I am a new creation in Christ. My heart and mind are being renewed day by day. Help me to believe this and live my life accordingly.

I pray that I will let go of all labels except this one: child of God.

You were taught, with regard to your former way of life, to put off your old self, which is being corrupted by its deceitful desires; to be made new in the attitude of your minds; and to put on the new self, created to be like God in true righteousness and holiness.

EPHESIANS 4:22-24

A Cup of Forgiveness

Forgiveness is such a beautiful thing. It's like a cup of water to someone dying of thirst. I am a truly blessed person because you have erased all my sins.

I need to stop and meditate on forgiveness more often. I need to be more grateful. I praise you from the depths of my soul for your mercy toward me and all your people.

It blows my mind that you love me so much, but I'm so grateful that you do. Amen.

Listen to my cry,
for I am in desperate need;
rescue me from those who pursue me,
for they are too strong for me.
Set me free from my prison,
that I may praise your name.

PSALM 142:6-7

Missing the Mark

———

I know that being honest and facing up to my own failures is vital to my spiritual health. I don't want to live in denial about the hurt I have caused for you, for others, and (inevitably) for myself. In light of your holiness, I deeply regret doing and saying things I shouldn't, and neglecting to do or say the right thing at the right time.

I am grateful for the Bible's reassurance that you are kind and compassionate. When I confess my mistakes, I am forgiven. That's why I am coming to you now. I am sorry for the ways I have missed the mark. Please forgive me and help me get past my guilt and shame.

I praise you for being such a forgiving God.

> I am writing to you, dear children, because your
> sins have been forgiven on account of his name.
>
> **1 JOHN 1:12**

Forgiving and Forgetting

―――――

Lord of mercy, as I review my recent past, I realize how many times I reacted foolishly. How many times I said something or did something without thinking about the consequences. I know I should pray, think, and seek sound advice, but I don't always take the time to do any of those things.

There are so many moments I wish I could forget. But I am grateful that you forgive me. I don't want my head to hit the pillow at night until things are right between you and me. I want to take the time to clear the air, to clear my mind and heart. My relationship with you means the world to me even though my actions don't always reflect that.

Thank you for loving me just the way I am. Your love inspires me to give you my all, to learn from my mistakes, and simply to be better tomorrow than I was today.

You are my friends if you do what I command.

JOHN 15:14

Finding Rest in Forgiveness

———

Lord, I have failed you again. This happens so many times that I wonder why you keep taking me back into your good graces.

But that's what you do, regardless of what I have done. Please give me the honesty to admit my sins. Give me the strength to accept whatever negative consequences come my way.

Most of all, show me your unlimited forgiveness. Let me find rest and peace in that forgiveness. Please point the way back to you. I commit to following better, more closely, this time.

> If we confess our sins, he is faithful and just and will forgive us our sins and purify us from all unrighteousness.
>
> **1 JOHN 1:9**

Pursued by Guilt

———

Guilt is hunting me like a wolf. It's relentless. I would do just about anything to escape it. And it feels like that wolf is feeding on my misery and fear.

Please assure me of your forgiveness. I want to focus on you, not my shame. Remind me of my secure future in you. You are with me in moments like these, moments when I wish I could crawl out of my own skin.

Let my soul find rest in your grace. Renew my sense of hope. You have promised your forgiveness to those who seek it. I need to rest in that truth. I want to be led by your peace, not hunted by a predator called Guilt. I know that when I look to you, I will see the way forward.

Wash away all my iniquity
and cleanse me from my sin...
Cleanse me with hyssop, and I will be clean;
wash me, and I will be whiter than snow.

PSALM 51:2,7

COMMUNION
WITH GOD

God Is Our Refuge

Graduation. This is the season of life when thoughts turn to fresh starts and new horizons. As I gaze into my future, be close to me, my Lord and Savior. Help me to embrace the hopes, dreams, and opportunities, as well as face all the challenges and uncertainties that come with life after graduation.

Please transform my fears into victories. Empower me when my faith falters and becomes weak. Teach me your ways. Help me to love people the way you do. Give me the strength to live for you today and through all my tomorrows.

> Trust in him at all times, you people;
> pour out your hearts to him,
> for God is our refuge.

PSALM 62:8

Silent Wisdom

―――――

I have to admit I don't feel that close to you right now. Sometimes I find myself waiting for an answer or a word of encouragement from you, but you seem to be silent.

At times like these, help me to realize that even when I don't hear you speaking, you are still near. I think about how a parent or a best friend doesn't always need to talk to me to make me feel better. Sometimes, it's enough to know someone is *there*. And you are the ultimate Father, the ultimate friend. You are always there for me. Thank you for your presence. I need to appreciate it more than I do.

And in those silent moments, may my mind and heart be open to what I can learn and experience. Sometimes silence can hold a wealth of wisdom for me.

Let the peace of Christ rule in your hearts, since as members of one body you were called to peace.

COLOSSIANS 3:15

Surrounded by God

Heavenly Father, I thank you for going before me. Help me to sleep well, wake up with hope, and begin my day with purpose.

I thank you for walking beside me. Please travel with me wherever today takes me. Calm my mind and reassure my heart, especially when I feel tired or troubled.

I thank you for being the support beneath me. Please catch me when I fall, and speak words of comfort to me if I start to panic.

I thank you for being above me. I lift my eyes to your goodness and power. I trust in your promises. Give me the strength to hold on to your Word even when my faith wobbles and wavers.

Lord, you make all things new. You are my Creator. You are forever nurturing, renewing, and growing those who love and follow you.

Thank you, and amen.

> God is Spirit, so those who worship him
> must worship in spirit and in truth.
>
> **JOHN 4:24 NLT**

A Personal God

———

My heavenly Father, thank you for being such a personal God. Sometimes I feel so close to you that I can sense you kneeling beside me when I pray. You see the tears no one else sees. You know the hidden fears lurking deep in my heart. You know the pain I won't reveal to anyone else. Above all, you see the good in me even when I see only my flaws.

Thank you for wrapping your arms around me and assuring me of your love and forgiveness. Help me show this forgiveness to others rather than judging them or putting them down. Help me to love people and to leave the judging to you.

This is how we know who the children of God are and who the children of the devil are: Anyone who does not do what is right is not God's child; nor is anyone who does not love their brother and sister.

1 JOHN 3:10

The Nature of Prayer

———

Dear wise Father, you understand me. I can share anything with you. My most terrifying thoughts. My darkest emotions. What's more, you know the call of my heart even when I can't seem to organize my thoughts or feelings into a prayer. Whatever is going on in my life, you are near.

Please remind me that prayer is about listening as well. Help me to quiet my mind and heart so I can learn what you are communicating to me. I know that you long for an open heart. May my heart be open when I pray to you and during all moments of my life.

May the Lord answer you when you are in distress;
may the name of the God of Jacob protect you...
May he give you the desire of your heart
and make all your plans succeed.

PSALM 20:1,4

The Message Matters

You will go to great lengths to communicate with your people. Extraordinary lengths. You spoke to Moses from a flaming bush. When a man named Balaam wanted to make the right choice, you inspired his donkey to say a few words to lead him in the right direction.

There are no limits to what you will do to communicate with us, with me. Of course, sometimes you speak quietly. It's the message that matters, not the medium. Let my ears—and my heart—be open to what you want to communicate to me.

God has said, "Never will I leave
you; never will I forsake you."

HEBREWS 13:5

The Privilege of Prayer

———

D ear God, thank you for inventing prayer. I know I am going to be praying a *lot* in the coming days, months, and years. Thank you for always being ready to hear from me. In fact, you actually invite and encourage me to talk with you.

And so I will. Every day. (Multiple times a day when I face an especially hard challenge.) I need to come to you as I strive to be the person you designed me to be. I will always be grateful for your unbreakable promise that you hear my prayers. You are God, and you never cover your ears. You care about me and about what is on my mind and on my heart.

> Hear my cry, O God;
> listen to my prayer.
>
> **PSALM 61:1**

MAKING AN IMPACT

Being an Example

I am young, but that doesn't mean I can't be an example for others. Help me live a life that draws people to you. As I look at the world around me, I realize that many of the people who claim to follow you aren't actually living as Jesus would. Of course, none of us is perfect. But I want you to shine through me even though I often make mistakes and sometimes speak carelessly.

I want others to be blessed by my example. I want them to see that I truly love you and honor you, even in the face of my inevitable failures.

I want to point people to you. Give me what I need to do just that. I ask this in your holy name. Amen.

May your hand be ready to help me,
for I have chosen your precepts.

PSALM 119:173

Speaking Truth

————

As I move into this new phase of my life, I pray that I will continue to speak out for truth and goodness when I need to. I have to admit that I stress out at the thought of being called hateful, intolerant, or pushy, but I want to do and say what is right regardless of the consequences.

When I need to speak out for you, Lord, help me to be humble, thoughtful, and reasonable. I know what it's like to be showered with your grace and mercy. I want that experience to inform what I say and how I say it.

Help me to remember that warning people about making mistakes is ultimately a kind act. So is standing up against powerful people who are abusing their influence and hurting those who are vulnerable. Give me the courage to (lovingly!) say what is true rather than what is politically correct.

Whatever you do, work at it with all your heart, as working for the Lord, not for human masters.

COLOSSIANS 3:23

The Spirit of Grace

I know you are not pleased when I become more focused on religious rules than on people. There are so many people who are needy—spiritually and in many other ways too. When I look at my world, I see people who need rescue and healing. They don't need to be reminded of how they don't measure up to religious standards.

I need to remember stories like the ones about the prodigal son and the good Samaritan. Stories about the kind of religion that pleases you.

Let me be an instrument of your life-changing grace and mercy, especially to those who are hurting or calling out from a deep pit of despair. Help me be as gracious to them as you have been to me. Amen.

You then, my child, be strengthened by
the grace that is in Christ Jesus.

2 TIMOTHY 2:1 ESV

A Love Revolution

─────────

I pray that everyone in my circle of influence, small though it may be, will see your love and grace in what I say and, more importantly, in what I do. I want to start a love revolution, even if it's a small one. I know that my "life toolkit" isn't complete yet, so please provide the tools I need. Help me to be the person you created me to be.

I think of friends and family who have helped show me better ways to live. I want to be this kind of influence for others. Please help me in this effort.

> The words of the reckless pierce like swords,
> but the tongue of the wise brings healing.

PROVERBS 12:18

Hungry, Homeless Jesus?

Dear Lord Jesus, as I embark on a new leg of my life's journey, I am encountering many new people. Remind me that all these people are your children. Help me to see you in the poor, the hungry, the homeless, and the outcast.

Remind me that I am supposed to help care for "the least of these." I am supposed to see *you* in the wounded eyes of the people whom much of society does not care about.

Show me how to minister to those in need. I will remember that when I attend to those needs, I'm doing it for you.

The King will reply, "Truly I tell you, whatever you did for one of the least of these brothers and sisters of mine, you did for me."

MATTHEW 25:40

Every Life Matters

———

Every life has influence, even mine. Every life has power. I pray that you will harness and direct the power you have given me. I know that other people are counting on me, praying for me, and hoping the best for me. I don't want to disappoint them. I don't want to disappoint you.

I want the power in my life to be flexed, not for my own good or my own ego, but for the good of others and for your glory, my Lord and my God. I praise you for being the source of everything good in me. Amen.

As God's chosen people, holy and dearly loved, clothe yourselves with compassion, kindness, humility, gentleness, and patience. Bear with each other and forgive one another if any of you has a grievance against someone. Forgive as the Lord forgave you.

COLOSSIANS 3:12-13

Giving with Love

———

Dear giver of all good things, I want to be a giving person, but I don't know what I have to offer. I'm just starting out, and I really don't have much. I am reminded of this every time I check my bank account balance.

Remind me how Jesus praised a woman who gave only two small coins as a temple offering. She was honored because she gave all she had. Help me remember that you are not impressed by how much money or other stuff I give. Generosity is measured by the size of our hearts. When we give with love, it matters. It could be a few coins, some clothes I haven't worn lately, my time, or my talent. I know you can use what I give to do something significant.

All I need to do is be as generous as I can. I commit to doing just that.

> Whoever has the gift of giving to
> others should give freely.
>
> **ROMANS 12:8 NCV**

An Instrument of Grace

———

Gracious God, it has been too long since I thanked you for the unbelievable privilege of being an instrument of your grace. I think grace is especially sweet when I get to deliver it to the very young, the poor, the elderly, or anyone whom society might neglect or take advantage of.

It is an honor to follow in the footsteps of Jesus, who seemed to be a magnet for the neediest people. I want to imitate him. I want to bring his love to my world. And I hope and pray that I can inspire others to follow his example as well.

I know that all of us can have an impact on the world if we act in the name of Jesus.

Love does not delight in evil but rejoices
with the truth. It always protects, always
trusts, always hopes, always perseveres.

1 CORINTHIANS 13:6-7

Our Hands Are God's Hands

I am amazed every time I think about the way you, the powerful and wise God of the universe, choose people like me to get your work done. The Bible assures us that we are your hands and feet.

What an honor—but at the same time, what a responsibility! We are your tools (in the best sense of the word) who feed the hungry, share the good news, comfort the hurting, encourage the discouraged, and protect the persecuted.

Please give me the courage and the strength to always be up to the task at hand—*your* hand!

Never walk away from someone who deserves help;
your hand is God's hand for that person.

PROVERBS 3:27 MSG

IN SEARCH OF HOPE

Living in Hope

It takes a lot of hard work and a lot of prayer to graduate. It's an accomplishment, and most of the time, I feel good about reaching such an important milestone in my life.

On the other hand, there is still that fear of failure. It hovers over me like a storm cloud. I am haunted by questions, such as "You reached one milestone, but what if you can't reach the next one?"

I don't want fears like this to hold me back from living the full life you want for me. I want to live boldly, not fearfully. Forgive me for the times my faith has grown weak. From this moment, I want to live hopefully. I know some failures will come, but with your help, I can overcome them. I can be an imperfect person and still reach my goals. Besides, I know that I tend to learn more from my failures than from my successes. That's not a cliché—it's a reality.

Help me to avoid comparing myself to those around me. That's the kind of thing that can feed fear. Instead, help me to pursue your unique plan for my life. Help me to remember that when I fail, your grace still shines.

> May the LORD our God be with us as he was with our ancestors; may he never leave us nor forsake us. May he turn our hearts to him, to walk in obedience to him.
>
> **1 KINGS 8:57-58**

Hopeful Eyes

———

As a child born of your Spirit, I want to praise you. I celebrate being one of your children. In you, I find healing, forgiveness, and power. I find mercy and peace. You have helped me reach this milestone in my life. I look ahead with hope—sometimes mixed with uncertainty and anxiety.

I need to remember how you have brought me to this point in my life. I have a few battle scars, even at my young age, but I look to the future with hopeful eyes. And that is because I am yours. Thank you for being my heavenly father. It's an honor to be your child.

> You made all the delicate, inner parts of my body
> and knit me together in my mother's womb.
> Thank you for making me so wonderfully complex!
> Your workmanship is marvelous—how well I know it.
>
> **PSALM 139:13-14 NLT**

Living Inside Grace

God of mercy, forgive me (again!) for losing my focus. Forgive me for letting problems and distractions overshadow your presence in my life. Thank you for your patience with me at times like this. Thank you for wrapping me in your grace.

I want to live inside your grace all the days of my life. Help me keep my mind and my heart focused on you. I praise and thank you for your forgiveness. You give me hope to go on. Amen.

> My grace is sufficient for you, for my
> power is made perfect in weakness.
>
> **2 CORINTHIANS 12:9**

Looking Forward

———

Gracious God, thank you for loving me as I am—bruised, broken, and bearing the marks of life's battles. I praise you because I don't have to be whole or perfect to be valuable in your eyes. When I am afraid to look in the mirror, you look on me with loving eyes. You help me look forward with hope rather than looking over my shoulder with regret.

And just as I don't have to be perfect to be accepted by you, I don't have to be perfect to be effective for you. I can help other people who are imperfect just like me. We help to make each other whole, knowing that one day you will make everyone and everything whole.

Where God's love is, there is no fear,
because God's perfect love drives out fear.

1 JOHN 4:18 NCV

Grace in Hard Times

God of hope, sometimes I feel that sadness is hovering above me wherever I go. People say things like "This too shall pass," but I wonder, "When? *Now* would be good!"

At times like this, it's hard to see how things will work out, how problems will be solved. Help me to remember that you are my deliverer. You will come through for me. You always do. You have provided comfort and encouragement for me in the past, and I know that your love and strength never run dry.

I pray for the grace to endure hard times, especially when it seems there is no quick fix. Sometimes life is like that. Let me learn from difficulties. Perhaps they can help me become a more compassionate person. Perhaps they will help me be more like Jesus. Amen.

Be joyful in hope, patient in affliction, faithful in prayer.

ROMANS 12:12

FINDING HEALING

A Spirit Renewed

———

I am hurting right now. It's a spiritual hurt because I feel bad for so many things I have said and done. I confess all this to you right now. Please forgive me. Please help me feel accepted, completely and unconditionally.

I give all my pain and disappointment to you. Create in me the kind of healing that renews my spirit and restores my strength. Help me to follow you with patience, as I know that healing can take time.

I commit to serving you. Thank you for caring for me and for always listening to my prayers.

Those who hope in the LORD
will renew their strength.
They will soar on wings like eagles;
they will run and not grow weary,
they will walk and not be faint.

ISAIAH 40:31

OUTGROWING GRUDGES

God, I feel like I should have outgrown grudges by now, but I still find myself withholding forgiveness from people. I don't want to live this way. I want to be a forgiving person. I want to make things right with any friend or family member who has offended me or hurt me.

In my own humanly imperfect way, I want to emulate the way you have forgiven me. You have forgiven me completely, without conditions.

Help me forgive the people I know I need to forgive. And please reveal to me any unresolved situations where forgiveness is needed but is being withheld. Whether I need to forgive someone or be forgiven myself, I want to make things right.

Get rid of all bitterness, rage and anger, brawling
and slander, along with every form of malice.

EPHESIANS 4:31

Grace Heals

———

Dear Lord, I come to you today with a heart full of regret. I have said things and done things that have hurt someone. I thought I could simply ask your forgiveness and move on with my life. After all, I am a graduate. I want to look forward, not backward. But I am feeling the pain of wounds that are not healing.

Help me understand that forgiveness is a process, not just a quick prayer. Help me clearly see what I can do to keep bringing healing to this situation. I pray for the courage to make a call, write a letter or email, or arrange for some face time. Show me what to say, what to do, and how to do it.

I praise you for providing grace. I know your grace can heal all the souls involved here. I truly want to be an instrument of this grace. Blessed be your name.

Let the beloved of the Lord rest secure in him,
for he shields him all day long,
and the one the Lord loves
rests between his shoulders.

DEUTERONOMY 33:12

Healing Wounds

———

Father God, even at a young age, I can look at my life and see how I have been damaged by sin. At times that sin was my own. At times, other people's poor decisions and thoughtless actions have left their marks on me.

Regardless of the source, I ask you to heal me from the damage that has been done. Show me how to rise above the pain and bitterness. Help me to forgive anyone I need to forgive. Grant me the courage I need to get rid of anything that is dragging me down, robbing me of my hopes and dreams for my life.

I acknowledge that I have been living with unhealed wounds for too long. I need your grace to heal me and make me whole again. So I am reaching out to you right now. Thank you for being so close to me.

Keep yourselves safe in God's love.

JUDE 1:21 NLT

God's Healing Touch

———

Thank you for the many ways you have taken care of me and provided for me. So many times, you have met my needs even before I realized exactly what I needed!

Right now I am asking you to bring your healing touch to my mind, body, and spirit. I don't feel quite right…I am not sure why, but you do. I want to be completely well.

Help me so I can serve you better. Give me patience, courage, honesty, and humility. Please give me whatever I am lacking right now. I thank you for hearing my prayers, now and always. Amen.

When you draw close to God, God
will draw close to you.

JAMES 4:8 TLB

MAKING WISE CHOICES

A Clear Conscience
Is a Soft Pillow

———

It feels so good to go through life without guilt dragging me down. I pray that in all I do, I will live a life that honors you and builds up the people I encounter. I know that a clear mind leads to a clean conscience, so I pray for your vision and direction in my life.

Help me to act and speak truthfully in all circumstances—even when it makes me look bad. I know that you ultimately bless those who do the right thing, but I don't want to think about earning blessings. I want to do the right thing simply because it's the right thing. Goodness and integrity are rewards in themselves. Thank you for providing Jesus as the ultimate example for me to follow.

The quiet words of the wise are more to be heeded than the shouts of a ruler of fools.

ECCLESIASTES 9:17

Every Day Matters

I am amazed every time I think about how you know the number of my days here on earth. There are times I wish I knew this too, but what I really want is to live for you every single day. I want to live as if every day matters—because it does.

Please make me useful. Reveal your purpose for me. Give me the strength and wisdom to do whatever you want me to do.

Thank you for the chance to serve you by serving others. I pray that they will see your love and grace as I go about the tasks of daily life. And when I do something well, I want people to see that it's you working in my life that makes good things happen. I give you all the glory, in the awesome name of Jesus.

As for me, I watch in hope for the Lord,
I wait for God my Savior;
my God will hear me.

MICAH 7:7

Courageous Choices

The older I get, the decisions I have to make seem to get harder and harder. Almost every choice I make carries the weight of huge potential consequences, both good and bad. I don't want fear or eagerness to overshadow God's will.

Let me look for guidance in the right places. Keep my ears open to your voice. Let me see clearly the path you show me in your perfect timing. Especially at times like this, I need wisdom beyond my own.

I ask you for the clarity to know which choice is right. I ask for courage to follow through even when the right path also looks like the most difficult one.

People with integrity walk safely,
but those who follow crooked paths will be exposed.

PROVERBS 10:9 NLT

Lighting the Way

———

Choices abound for me. As a young grad, I face more choices than ever before. However, in this new chapter of my life, there might not be as many people nearby to help me make the best choices. This is both good and bad. I know I need to accept more decision-making responsibility. This is a time for me to discover what I truly believe and to continue to establish my own identity.

On the other hand, I realize that the quality of my life is a direct product of the choices I make. Please help me to seek and find the information, wisdom, and perspective to choose wisely. And remind me that following the Bible's time-tested principles helps to ensure my protection, fulfillment, and well-being. You are *for* me, as are the guidelines you have provided in your Word. So above all else, I choose to follow you.

Your word is a lamp for my feet,
a light on my path.

PSALM 119:105

DECISION TIME

———

This is a time of new beginnings, a time of decisions that I must make—or someone else might make them for me. I commit to being an active participant in my life, not just a spectator. Guide me and help me choose the right paths.

Please open my eyes so I can see clearly what is right for me. Help me choose truth and goodness. Help me avoid greed and pride. Please bring out the best in me as I travel through life with you as my guide and my strength.

> In the morning, LORD, you hear my voice;
> in the morning I lay my requests before you
> and wait expectantly.

PSALM 5:3

Too Busy?

As I look at what's in store for me after graduation, I realize I could be entering the busiest time of my life. I know I need to focus on my goals and new responsibilities. However, I don't want to become so busy or so focused on myself that I can't find time to provide support to those who need it.

I want to be a willing servant, ready to provide a helping hand or a listening ear. I want to be attuned to others' needs. I want to be as generous as possible with my resources. With your power and wisdom, I can be gracious and helpful to those around me. I want to welcome others the way you have welcomed me.

Grow in the grace and knowledge of our
Lord and Savior Jesus Christ. To him
be glory both now and forever!

2 PETER 3:18

PERSONAL GROWTH

Growing with God

———

Dear God, thank you for always being there for me. I feel amazed every time I think about how you know everything about me and yet still love me. I can't honestly say that about anyone else in my life.

I know I need to connect with you more often and more deeply. I commit to doing this. I know I will need your help. Create in me a hunger to spend more time with you. Help me be patient as I try to become a more spiritual person. (You know how I can get frustrated when prayer doesn't come easily or when I have trouble connecting with a passage from the Bible.)

Let me find more joy in your presence. Let me put my fears aside and grow closer to you, my Lord and my God.

Let love and faithfulness never leave you.

PROVERBS 3:3

A PERSON OF PRAYER

Dear God, I want to become a person of prayer. I want communication with you to become a natural part of my life, just like eating or breathing. I thank you for always being ready to hear from me. In fact, you actually invite and encourage me to talk with you. How amazing is that?

May I always remember to come to you as I strive to be the person you designed me to be. I will always be grateful for your unbreakable promise to hear my prayers. You care about me and what is on my mind and on my heart. Amen.

> Whoever serves me must follow me; and
> where I am, my servant also will be. My
> Father will honor the one who serves me.
>
> **JOHN 12:26**

The Lord of Every Day

I know that each new chapter of my life gives me a chance to grow spiritually as well as in other ways. I pray that I will take advantage of every opportunity to become a spiritual person, a person of depth and understanding.

Not all great moments of spiritual awakening have to happen inside a church (though many of them do). So help me to avoid limiting you. You are able to speak to me during a quiet walk in the park. Or over coffee with a good-hearted friend. Or while I am out volunteering for a cause I believe in. May I never put you in a box labeled "Open Only on Sundays." I want you to be the Lord of every day, every circumstance.

Since we are receiving a Kingdom that is
unshakable, let us be thankful and please God
by worshiping him with holy fear and awe.

HEBREWS 12:28 NLT

A Faith Dabbler?

Loving Jesus, I feel as if I disappoint you in so many ways. I neglect my prayer time and Bible study time. I tend to separate my spiritual life from my everyday life. I sometimes act as if you and I were strangers, not friends.

Give me a hunger to know you better. Let me meditate on you and your words. Let me pray—not just when I need something, but all the time. We must keep our lines of communication open. (And when I say we, I mean *me*.)

Open my eyes so that I will see your hand and your heart in the people and events that fill my life. Help me to stop dabbling in my faith and embrace it with my whole heart.

> You make known to me the path of life;
> you will fill me with joy in your presence,
> with eternal pleasures at your right hand.
>
> **PSALM 16:11**

Soul Food

———

Today I am grateful for soul food. I love the way your Word feeds my soul. It's amazing how a Scripture verse, a song, or a few words from a sermon can give me strength and wisdom for the day. You seem to know just what I need to hear, what I need to remember.

As my life gets busier and more complicated, I know I will need that soul food more than ever. Keep me hungry for your knowledge and perspective.

When I skip a physical meal, I can get irritable, tired, or irrational. Sometimes I get a massive headache. The same kind of thing can happen when I neglect to feed my soul. Thank you for an endless supply of good spiritual nourishment. May I never forget to take it in.

Crave pure spiritual milk, so that by it you
may grow up in your salvation, now that
you have tasted that the Lord is good.

1 PETER 2:23

LOVE AND ROMANCE

A Prayer for Purity

————

Father, I live in a world that provides such easy access to all kinds of sexual immorality. I know that some older adults would freak out if they knew how easily my generation can take advantage of the temptations that surround us every day.

I pray for a mature, big-picture perspective when it comes to all things sexual. Help me take to heart the long-term devastation that results from a few moments of empty pleasure. I don't want that kind of shame and wreckage in my life. I want a real, loving relationship, not a cheap imitation of any kind.

Help me to be a discerning person. Help me to be honest with myself about my weaknesses so that I don't put myself in situations where I am likely to make big mistakes.

Help me to find friendships where I can encourage others and they can encourage me. Where we can call each other on our rationalizations and excuses. Open the doors to honest sharing.

In short, please keep my mind and my body pure—and under your control. Amen.

It is God's will that you should be sanctified: that
you should avoid sexual immorality; that each of
you should learn how to control your own body in a
way that is holy and honorable, not in passionate
lust like the pagans, who do not know God.

1 THESSALONIANS 4:3-5

Leaning on God

————

Few things in life bring more joy—yet more pain—than close relationships. Whether it's a deep friendship or a romance, it's scary when my happiness is intertwined with someone else's.

I don't know what graduation will mean for this special relationship in my life. (You know the one.) It's tempting to keep playing worst-case scenarios in my head and sinking into despair as a result.

Help me to trust you regardless of the outcome of this relationship. Things might get better, but they might get worse. Whatever the case, I pray for the peace that you alone can provide. Help me to draw my strength and hope from your endless supply.

Thank you for walking through this uncertain time with me. Draw me to your side. Let me lean on you. No matter what comes, I will love you and praise you for being in the thick of it with me. What an amazing God you are!

Teach me, and I will be quiet;
show me where I have been wrong.

JOB 6:24

GUIDANCE AND
DIRECTION

The Way Everlasting

Loving Creator, I thank you for making each person a unique reflection of your image. I feel amazed every time I think of how I get to be part of something much bigger than myself—without sacrificing my individuality.

With this truth in mind, I humbly ask you,

> Open my eyes to your wonders.
> Open my mind to your truths.
> Open my life to your purpose.
> Open my heart to receive your love—
> and to share it every day.
> Amen.

> Search me, God, and know my heart;
> test me and know my anxious thoughts.
> See if there is any offensive way in me,
> and lead me in the way everlasting.

PSALM 139:23-24

When Life Is a Maze

I have to admit it; I'm confused. I feel as if I'm trapped in a maze. What seemed like the road to success yesterday has turned out to be today's dead end.

I'm so thankful that you are above it all. If life is a maze, you can see the whole thing, not just confusing bits and pieces. You know where I need to go—and which paths I would be wise to avoid. Help me to shift my focus away from the confusion that's in my face right now and look to you instead.

I know that your wisdom never falters. And though I sometimes make wrong turns, your mercies are renewed every day. Thank you for being my patient guide.

Seek his will in all you do,
and he will show you which path to take.

PROVERBS 3:6 NLT

A Life That Counts

―――――

I want to do your will, Lord, but I don't always know what your will is. As I face some important decisions about my future, I ask for your direction. I don't want to bargain with you, and I don't want to make a commitment I can't keep.

I want to dedicate my future to loving and serving you and your people. How I accomplish that is up to you. I trust in your wisdom and power. I know that you hold my life in your hands. I want to make my life matter. I want to bring honor to your name. Help me discover, day by day, how to accomplish these goals.

Do not judge, and you will not be judged. Do not condemn, and you will not be condemned. Forgive, and you will be forgiven. Give, and it will be given to you.

LUKE 6:37-38

Love Perseveres

———

Merciful God, may nothing separate me from you today. Help me to think, speak, and act in obedience to your Word, not by my own whims or according to outside influences. I want to keep my heart pure and my mind clear.

Protect me from the traps of carelessness and selfishness. Let me see each opportunity to serve you as something to embrace rather than an inconvenience that interrupts my personal agenda.

I know I will miss the mark, but I pray that my mistakes won't distance me from you. When I mess up, that's when I need you most. Help me to feel your unconditional love in the deepest part of my heart. I am amazed every time I think about how you love me despite my faults. Let me draw strength and hope from your amazing love.

Give thanks to the Lord, for he is good;
his love endures forever.

1 CHRONICLES 16:34

Saying Yes

———

Lord, with a humble heart, I thank you for the abilities and passions you have planted in me. I know I have weaknesses too (that's the humbling part), but I believe you have given me the tools I need to make something extraordinary out of my life. I'm confident I can contribute positive things to my world.

I know that sometimes a talent can seem like a burden because of all the expectations from myself and others. Forgive me for the times I have failed to develop my skills or put them into action. Forgive me for the times I have ignored your efforts to lead me.

From this point on, I want to say yes to every opportunity to put my God-given gifts to work. I want to answer your call. I want to share your goodness every chance I get.

Fan into flame the gift of God, which is in you.

2 TIMOTHY 1:6

We're Next

I notice that a lot is being said about my generation. Not all of it is good, and sometimes our critics just might have a point. So I pray today for my generation. I pray that we will do great things for you—as well as little, everyday things that reflect your goodness.

I pray that we will learn from the generations ahead of us. We must draw from their wisdom and experience, but we must also learn from their errors and shortcomings. May we rise up boldly to the challenges we face.

We are the world's next doctors, teachers, political leaders, missionaries, soldiers, counselors, and pastors. We are the authors, reformers, and parents of the future. Heavenly Father, we are your next church. Please use us to do your will.

We are God's handiwork, created in
Christ Jesus to do good works, which God
prepared in advance for us to do.

EPHESIANS 2:10

THE QUEST FOR
PEACE AND REST

A Heart at Peace

––––––––

My prayer for today is simple: Deliver me from busyness. I don't need to fill every single day with assignments completed, money earned, or items checked off a to-do list.

A day to reflect, pray, and dream—that is a gift! There are days when I would be wise to simply let your peace fill my soul, heal my soul.

Experiencing peace of mind and spirit is an achievement in itself. This kind of peace chases away despair and prepares me for what lies ahead. In my crowded life, help me find room to breathe, to meditate on you, to seek a peace that surpasses all understanding.

A peaceful heart leads to a healthy body.

PROVERBS 14:30 NLT

Wrapped in Peace

———

My prayer today is simple: I need rest. Please wrap me in peace and calm so I can refresh my tired mind and body. I want to face tomorrow with renewed strength and a clear mind. Thank you for the many ways you have blessed my life. I know I need to count these blessings instead of counting worries.

I love being your child. I want to be a faithful child, and that can be extra difficult when I am exhausted. Please grant me the simple blessing of a good night's sleep. (Perhaps even a good afternoon's nap?) May your presence provide peace and safety. May I awake with renewed energy and a fresh supply of heavenly love to share. Please help me to rest, assured of your care for me.

> May the Lord answer you when you are in distress;
> may the name of the God of Jacob protect you.
>
> **PSALM 20:1**

A Heavy Heart

God of all strength, my heart is heavy right now, and I feel as if I'm carrying a huge burden alone. I'm overwhelmed and exhausted. I have heard people say, "Let God carry your load," but I am not sure how to do this. Will you show me how? Please take this load off of me somehow.

Bless me with rest. Help me to sleep and to wake up with a lighter heart. I need your strength every day, but especially on days like this. Thank you for hearing me.

Come to me, all you who are weary and
burdened, and I will give you rest.

MATTHEW 11:28

Blessed with Rest

———————

Dear God, I am so tired in every way. Please bless me with rest tonight. A simple good night's sleep would make such a positive difference in my life right now. Forgive me for anything I have done that did not honor you. I know I will sleep better when my conscience is clear.

Thank you for knowing me so well and loving me so much anyway. I need your help every day. (Who doesn't?) With you, even the hardest challenge is doable. Please bless my friends and family. I know so many of them are tired too. May we find rest and protection in you.

Hope does not put us to shame, because God's love has been poured out into our hearts through the Holy Spirit, who has been given to us.

ROMANS 5:5

Peace of Mind

My patient God, I wonder how many times I have prayed while wondering if you were hearing me. You know better than anyone how doubt crawls into my mind, especially when I am praying new prayers while still waiting for answers to older prayers.

Forgive me for entertaining doubt. Grant me the peace of mind and the strength to wait patiently. And open my eyes to those times when you might actually be answering a prayer, but I'm too stubborn or distracted to realize it!

I want to pray to you with more hope and less doubt. And I know I can't achieve this without you. Thank you for hearing this prayer—and all my other ones too.

> Surely your goodness and love will follow me
> all the days of my life, and I will dwell in
> the house of the Lord forever.

PSALM 23:6

In Search of Relief

———

Lord, today I ask you for a time and place of quiet. Please help me shut out the distractions and busyness. I need time to think. I need time to reflect on my life so far. I need to thank you for what you have done and are doing right now for me. And I need to pray thoughtfully for people in my life who need prayer. I want to take the time to really pray rather than mumbling a few quick words before moving on to some other task.

Quietness brings relief. It brings the kind of deep contemplation that helps me grow spiritually and reset my priorities. My life moves too fast sometimes. Help me quiet my heart and mind. Let me simply be present with you. Amen.

In repentance and rest is your salvation;
in quietness and trust is your strength.

ISAIAH 30:15

Paths to Peace

Dear God, I know I can experience your peace when I focus on you more than I do on anyone or anything else. I experience your peace when I pray for you to calm my heart. When I find someone to talk with me and listen to me. There are many paths to peace…as long as you are with me on that path. Because wherever you are, your peace is there too.

May your voice be clearer than all the noise surrounding me. That's the voice I want to follow, the one that encourages me toward the paths that lead to good things. Let me hear your voice above the criticisms of others, above my own fears and insecurities.

Create in me a pure heart, O God,
and renew a steadfast spirit within me.

PSALM 51:10

OUR FAITHFUL GOD

An Awesome Promise

Father God, what an awesome promise you have given to us—the promise that says you will use everything that happens in this life for the good of those who love you. In my young life, I have already seen this promise come true. Certainly, not everything that has happened to me has been good. But I am always amazed at how you can bring good things from bad situations. Even awful situations.

I take comfort in this promise. Thank you for what you do for me and for all your people. I will continue to believe in you and the way you can guide my life.

> We know that all things work together for
> good to those who love God, to those who
> are called according to His purpose.
>
> **ROMANS 8:28 NKJV**

LOVE ENDURES FOREVER

Caring Father, there is nothing like your amazing and enduring love. Your love fills me up and holds me together—even when the world around me seems to be falling to pieces. When I feel weak, I know that you have my back. You sustain me with a strength that is beyond my own.

When things are unraveling around me, help me keep it together. You've been my rock in so many hard times already. There have been times when I've thought, "I don't know if I can survive this." And yet here I am—thanks to you. I need to remember that. Remind me to rest in the strength of your forever love.

Give thanks to the LORD, for he is good.
His love endures forever.
Give thanks to the God of gods.
His love endures forever.
Give thanks to the Lord of lords:
His love endures forever.

PSALM 136:1-3

A Good, Good Father

Lord, when I open my mind and let myself dream about the future, I get pumped up. There are so many things I hope I can do in the days and years ahead. But then doubt starts to creep in. I wonder if I have what it takes. I wonder if I'll be able to handle the disappointments I know will come.

Remind me that you are a good Father. You want me to be fulfilled. You want me to have a life that's meaningful.

When I start to doubt, help me to remember that you are on my side and that you always have more than enough grace to help me handle any situation. Keep my dreams in tune with your will. I know we can accomplish great things…together.

Teach us to live wisely and well!

PSALM 90:12 MSG

FACING
UNCERTAINTY

Loving from the Center

I realize that moving ahead in life means leaving some things behind. For me, those things include what is familiar and comfortable to me. This can be scary, but it can be a good thing as well. Help me to remember that when some of the familiar trappings are removed, I can truly take stock of my life.

Help me distinguish what is solid rock under my feet and what is shifting sand.

I thank you for being my one constant in a rapid-fire, shape-shifting world. With you as my foundation, I know I can face anything.

Love from the center of who you are; don't fake it.

ROMANS 12:9 MSG

A Guide Named God

Heavenly Father, I am grateful that you are the great counselor, because I need your guidance right now. I face some big decisions, and I don't know what to do. Help me to know your will. Please send someone to show me the steps I need to take. I am depending on you.

Help me to have faith that you will provide what I need, when I need it. Help me to remember that what I want and what I truly need are not necessarily the same thing. I want to manage my time and my money wisely as I move forward into my future.

Thank you for providing for me. I need to remember how many times you have come through for me in the past. I know you will be my guide and my deliverer in the future as well.

The Lord is with me like a mighty warrior.

JEREMIAH 20:11

Clarity, Please?

———

What I wouldn't give for a little clarity right now. My to-do list is so overwhelming, I am afraid to look at it sometimes. Lord, as I start each day, please help me to find faith amid all the chaos.

I ask you for the desire and the ability to see you, hear you, talk with you, and give thanks to you. Please help me to draw nearer and nearer to you. I want my faith to grow. I want to understand you in new ways, deeper ways.

You are everything I could ever hope for. You have the strength and wisdom to help me find peace in the busy storm that is my life. I know that calming storms is one of your specialties.

> Love the Lord your God with all your heart and
> with all your soul and with all your strength.

DEUTERONOMY 6:5

THE WHAT-IFS

It's ironic how my graduation has generated as many questions as answers. So many what-if scenarios spin in my mind, I can start feeling dizzy. My friends and I have so many questions:

Will I make enough money to earn a living?

How long will it take me to pay off my student loans?

Should I pursue an advanced degree or jump immediately into the job market?

What will life be like outside my normal routine and comfort zone?

Sometimes I feel paralyzed by all the what-ifs. Lord, please keep me calm in the middle of the storm. Put a leash on my imagination when it threatens to run wild. Settle my mind and heart in that special sanctuary of calm that only you can provide.

Thank you for having a plan and purpose for my life. I know you will see me through, whatever the future may bring. Help me to focus on what I can do and should do at this moment. The rest…I leave in your strong hands. Amen.

Keep your lives free from the love of money and
be content with what you have, because God has
said, "Never will I leave you; never will I forsake you."

HEBREWS 13:5

New Mercies

I don't remember a time in my life when I was more uncertain. So many forks in the road, so many options for me to choose from! I don't know who or what will cross my path on any given day. But you are the rock—my rock-solid foundation. Teach me to stand strong in you, to choose your way.

Help me walk in truth rather than be pulled one way or the other by bad advice—or my own mixed-up emotions. Let me embrace every opportunity to grow as your child and to help others grow as well. In an uncertain world, you love me unconditionally. And that will never change.

Even if I fail today, speak love into my life. Remind me that your mercies are new every single morning. That amazes me. That makes me grateful.

Because of the Lord's great love we are not consumed,
for his compassions never fail.
They are new every morning;
great is your faithfulness.

LAMENTATIONS 3:22-23

A Safe Place

———

Dear Lord, with all my heart, I thank you for your kindness. It's like a magnet that pulls me closer to you. I feel blessed to have a God who wants a close relationship with me, a God who is approachable.

I'm not a kid anymore, but I know I still need a safe place. I need a place where I can take down all my defense mechanisms. I need a refuge where my soul can rest. You are that safe place for me. You are like a storm shelter when a tornado is ravaging everything else in sight.

In an uncertain world, I am sure that you love me. I am sure that I can find shelter from life's storms. Thank you.

I will never forget your precepts,
for by them you have preserved my life.

PSALM 119:93 NIV

Q&A

———

So many questions awaiting answers:

When can I move into my new place?

When will I hear back about the job interview?

Did I get into that special program I applied for?

Did I get approved for that loan?

Are things going to work out with that potential roommate?

I admit that I get tired of waiting for answers to questions like these. From the small stuff to the big stuff, it all wears down my patience. I wish I could snap my fingers and see all the pieces fall into place. But that is not real life.

And so I ask you, my Lord, to help me focus on what I can control and release the rest to you. Please help me remember all those times you have been faithful in the past. Those moments when your timing was perfect—even though I thought things were moving way too slowly.

I thank you for always being at work, often in ways I cannot see. And if there is something you need to build in me through all this, may my stubborn spirit be moldable. It's not always easy to say, "Not my will, but yours," but that is what I am saying. My life is in your hands, now and forever. Amen.

You do not have because you do not ask God.

JAMES 4:2

PATIENCE PAYS OFF

Your Time, Not Mine

———

Loving Father, as I leave to go "make it all happen," help me remember that I'm not really the one who makes it all happen. You are! As much as I want to work hard, hustle, and learn, let me not get far from the truth that you hold the universe in your hand. You hold every day in my future in your hand. You have it all under control.

I may not see the results for a while, but I know your plan is so good. Your plans are infinitely better than mine. And your timing is infinitely better than mine as well. As I struggle to make the right moves and the right decisions, help me be patient. And most of all, help me remember that while it might not look like things are happening for me, you are always moving, and you are always *for me.*

> By the grace of God I am what I am, and his grace to me was not without effect. No, I worked harder than any of them—yet not I, but the grace of God that was with me.
>
> **1 CORINTHIANS 15:10**

A Paucity of Patience

Please forgive me, Lord, for my lack of patience. When people see me trying to force my will upon life, what they *don't* see is my reliance on you. But I do rely on you. Big-time.

Being an adult requires more patience than I can muster on my own. I know I need your help. I thank you for the example of Jesus and other heroes of the faith. And I thank you for the adults in my life who have modeled maturity, faith, and yes, patience.

I pray for a more patient heart and a less frantic mind. I want to live life at your pace, no one else's.

> Wait for the Lord. Be strong and take
> heart and wait for the Lord.

PSALM 27:14

TACKLING
TEMPTATION

The Strength to Say No

———

Dear God, I am so glad you are strong—especially when I am not. I need your strength right now because I find myself being tempted to be involved in things I know are not good for my body, mind, or soul. Please give me the strength to say a polite but firm "no thanks" to the pressures. Battling temptation is especially hard when it comes from my friends. Help me to face this challenge with courage and sensitivity.

Help me find better things to occupy my time. Thank you for being my strength in this struggle. Thank you for understanding the temptations that can push me or pull me in the wrong direction. Whatever it takes for me to say no, that's what I ask, in Jesus' name. Amen.

I will conduct the affairs of my house
with a blameless heart.
I will not look with approval
on anything that is vile.

PSALM 101:2-3

Staying True

———

I am young, but I'm not that naive. I know that life after graduation will bring many challenges along with plenty of opportunities and good times.

I faced temptations before I graduated, and I know I will continue to face them now. So I ask you to protect me from sinful thoughts and actions. Deliver me from that pull that feels as strong as gravity itself.

Keep my eyes focused on you, my feet steady on the road you have called me to walk. I don't want temptation to knock me off course.

Let's face it—you know how weak I can be sometimes. That's why I am reaching out to you right now. Please deliver me from temptation. I need you. I know you can rescue me from all evil.

The Lord will be at your side
and will keep your foot from being snared.

PROVERBS 3:26

A Crowd of One

The desire to be part of the "it crowd" is something you never really outgrow. Like most people I know, I want to feel like I belong. I want to feel like I have a support group around me. But sometimes my crowd leads me into bad places. That's why Jesus is the ultimate role model. He wasn't afraid to stand alone, even to die alone.

Help me to stay faithful to you regardless of where everyone else is heading. Remind me that being friends with people and helping people does not mean I have to do everything they do or go everywhere they go. I know whom I need to follow. A crowd of just one.

Guard my life and rescue me;
do not let me be put to shame,
for I take refuge in you.

PSALM 25:20

A GIVING HEART

Sharing My Gifts

———

Like a lot of people my age, I am not afraid to share my opinions, especially from the relative safety of social media. (If I get a negative comment, I can just hide or delete it.)

But it's a different story when it comes to sharing something more personal, such as the emotions, fears, and beliefs I hold deep in my heart. I wonder how many of my peers are afraid to write a poem, draw a picture, or sing a song because they think their talents aren't worthy of anyone's attention. Or they don't want to be vulnerable and share what they truly think and feel deep inside. They fear what others might think of them. I know this fear quite well.

Please give me the courage to share my creativity and my heart. You don't expect me to be perfect. (Neither does anyone else—or at least *almost* anyone else!) If I write, speak, sing, or draw with sincerity, I know you will help me touch lives with my creativity.

As a father has compassion on his children,
so the LORD has compassion on those who fear him;
for he knows how we are formed,
he remembers that we are dust.

PSALM 103:13-14

The Gift of Prayer

Before I turn the page on this day, I want to pray for the people I love, especially those who are farther away now that graduation has happened. Whether they are near or far, may your love find them and touch them. Please heal their hurts and keep them safe.

For the ones who are struggling spiritually, please help them see you for who you really are. For those who are lonely, let them feel especially close to you right now.

I know I have my own needs and concerns, but it feels good to be able to take the focus off of me and put it on others. Thank you for the privilege of praying for my friends and family. It's a way I can reach out and touch them, even the ones who are far away. Thank you for loving all of us. Amen.

> Do not be anxious about anything, but in every situation, by prayer and petition, with thanksgiving, present your requests to God.
>
> **PHILIPPIANS 4:6**

A God Hug

Lord, I know so many people who are discouraged, confused, or just flat-out exhausted. I wonder how many people are feeling defeated right now, people in my life who are hiding their struggles as best they can.

I pray for all these people right now. Please strengthen them and encourage them, just as you have done for me so many times. Help them hold on to hope. Give them a God hug. Surround them with your love. I ask this in your loving name. Amen.

> The Lord protects and preserves all
> those who are loyal to him.
>
> **PSALM 31:23 TPT**

The Love Test

I have heard a lot and read a lot about what makes someone a true Christian. Your Word makes it clear to me. The badge of a true Christian should read LOVE. That's the true test.

I could recite the Bible from Genesis to Revelation or commit fewer sins than anyone around me, and it wouldn't mean anything without love. People might be impressed with knowledge or good behavior, but they are moved by love.

More than anything else, make me a loving person. Provide opportunities for me to show love and compassion and mercy to the people around me. I know that everything else I must be as a Christian is drawn from a wellspring of love. May I be a source of your amazing love. Amen.

We remember before our God and Father
your work produced by faith, your labor
prompted by love, and your endurance
inspired by hope in our Lord Jesus Christ.

1 THESSALONIANS 1:3

THE GOD OF
ALL COMFORT

A Comforting Presence

***

I get uncomfortable in environments filled with unfamiliar sights, sounds, and smells. I thought I might outgrow homesickness, but maybe that's something one never outgrows.

Please let me sense the comforting presence of your Spirit. I believe any place can be a good place if you are there with me.

At the same time, I realize that nothing will feel exactly like home, with all its familiar comforts. However, sometimes the best place for me is not the most comfortable place. Let me draw comfort from the fact that new surroundings are indicators of how my post-graduation life is progressing and how I am growing as a person.

Most of all, I thank you for being with me wherever I am. And thank you for preparing my ultimate home in heaven.

I will praise the LORD, who counsels me;
even at night my heart instructs me.

PSALM 16:7

Free Fall

Sometimes I feel like I'm in a free fall. The solid ground beneath my feet has disappeared, and it's hard to make sense out of anything that's going on in my life.

This is why I need to connect with you now. I know that I can hang on to you regardless of what is going on around me. I pray to you in all honesty because I know you can handle my darkest thoughts and my worst fears.

I ask for your comfort right now. I need to feel my feet back on solid ground. I need what only you can provide. Thank you for hearing this prayer. I trust in you. Amen.

Wisdom's instruction is to fear the LORD,
and humility comes before honor.

PROVERBS 15:33

A True Friend

———

Lord Jesus, sometimes I feel as if you are my only true friend. You are the only one who knows all my struggles and pain. Thank you for helping me carry a load that is sometimes too heavy for me to manage alone.

Thank you for listening to me with such amazing kindness and patience. You are always there for me. I can find you regardless of where I am or what I am going through. You never get tired of hearing me out. And you do more than listen to my troubles. You enter into them. You are right here with me, especially when I am hurting.

In an uncertain world, you are the one I can always turn to. I know nothing can separate me from your love. Nothing can rob me of your friendship. For this I am eternally grateful.

It is by grace you have been saved, through
faith—and this not from yourselves, it is the gift of
God—not by works, so that no one can boast.

EPHESIANS 2:8-9

KEEPING IT REAL

Clear Eyes

———

Lord Jesus, help me to see you more clearly. I want the fulfillment of an honest and deep relationship with you. I want you to be the center of my life.

I know I have disappointed you. I have neglected spending time with you. Sometimes I have avoided you. I often feel as if I'm pretending to be a Christian rather than actually being one. I know there is a huge difference between those two things. I am sorry for being so inconsistent. Give me the hunger to know you better through your Word, in prayer, and by spending time with people who live out their faith day by day. I want to see your hand at work. I want to feel your heart today and every day. Amen.

> The eyes of the Lord are on the righteous
> and his ears are attentive to their prayer.
>
> **1 PETER 3:12**

The Me in the Mirror

Sometimes when I look in the mirror, I don't like what I see. Occasionally that's because I'm not getting enough sleep, and it's starting to show. But at other times, it's because I'm embarrassed or ashamed about something I have done. At times like these, I don't want anyone to see me.

That's why I thank you for accepting me as I am and meeting me where I am. I don't have to climb to a spiritual peak to find you. And I don't have to pretend that nothing is wrong, especially on those days when almost *everything* is wrong. I am forever grateful that you love me as I am. But I'm equally grateful that your love makes me want to be all I can be.

You give me purpose. I feel valuable because to you, I *am* valuable.

We have this treasure in jars of clay to show that this all-surpassing power is from God and not from us.

2 CORINTHIANS 4:7

Adulthood 101

———

I wish there were a crash course on the ways of adulthood. I'm trying to adjust to a new role, but sometimes I feel as if I'm faking it—and not fooling anyone.

On days like today, when I don't know if I can play this confusing young-adult role for one more minute, help me find my way. Comfort me in my times of uncertainty. Direct me when I wander off track. Remind me that I need to live *my* version of young adulthood, not someone else's. It's okay if my life doesn't look exactly like someone else's. I want to focus on the things I do well and to learn and develop the skills I will need in the future.

More than anything else, may my life reflect the love and grace of my heavenly Father. Amen.

We all, who with unveiled faces contemplate
the Lord's glory, are being transformed into
his image with ever-increasing glory, which
comes from the Lord, who is the Spirit.

2 CORINTHIANS 3:18

HEALTH AND
WELL-BEING

THE TECHNOLOGY TRAP

Technology is a great, but it can be a trap. I don't want to get stuck stagnating behind a screen. Make me a person on the move. Let me run, walk, or wheel in the open air whenever I can. Let me celebrate simply being alive. What a gift that is! Thank you, Jesus. I want to enjoy your amazing gift of life.

And as I am out breathing the air, may my spirit feel as free as my body. Let me celebrate life. Let me savor life. Let me move to embrace the life you have given to me.

All my longings lie open before you, LORD.

PSALM 38:9

SABOTAGE

God, I know I will need to be healthy to overcome the challenges that life after graduation will bring. So I ask you to strengthen my mind and my body, just as you strengthen my soul. Help me avoid anything that sabotages my health: junk food, junk entertainment, or simple laziness.

Thank you for caring about my well-being. You have numbered the hairs on my head, so I know you care about the rest of me too. You created this body of mine, and you know all its intricacies. Help me to treat my body like the precious gift it is. May I never take it for granted.

> Guard my life, for I am faithful to you;
> save your servant who trusts in you.
> You are my God.

PSALM 86:2

LEADING AND
FOLLOWING

Looking for Leadership

I am grateful for all the people who have been leaders and strong examples to me so far in my life. With this in mind, I pray for the same kind of people for the next chapter of my life. Bring me people who will point me in the right direction. Bring me people who will help me to think clearly and act with integrity.

Please give me the humility to listen and the willingness to learn. I want to accept responsibility when I make a mistake. I know it won't be easy, but I pray I will gratefully welcome accountability in my life.

> If you quit listening, dear child…
> you'll soon be out of your depth.

PROVERBS 19:27 MSG

With Respect

———

Being a graduate does not mean I am completely independent. In fact, I might be responsible to even more people now. Bosses, landlords, mentors, teachers at the next educational level…a grad still has people to answer to.

Help me to remember that those I have to rely on or report to are people, just like me. They are going to have bad days. They are going to be rude or impatient at times. As I deal with these new people-related challenges, please remind me of your everlasting love. You see me, and you care about me. Help me to avoid the mistake of expecting too much of any flawed human being (that would be all of us). You are the only one who will never fail me.

Please help me release my hurt and anger when I feel I am treated unjustly. I place my "offenders" in your hands. I want to live in the freedom that forgiveness brings.

Do to others as you would have them do to you.

LUKE 6:31

Love at Work

———

Love is a wonderful concept. But it becomes more than a concept when I see people showing love in their daily lives. Thank you for the loving people you have placed in my life. People who show me how your Word works in the real world. They are like living sermons, living Bible studies. They are the hands of God. I pray that I can be this kind of person for others. I want to make others' lives better and happier.

I want to be a helping hand, a loving hand, in your name.

Be completely humble and gentle; be
patient, bearing with one another in love.

EPHESIANS 4:2

A Mouth Running Amok

Dear merciful God, I'm embarrassed (and sometimes ashamed) when I think about how many times my mouth has gotten ahead of my common sense. A few careless words, whether spoken or broadcast on social media, can hurt so many people.

I pray that my emotions won't get the best of me anymore. Help me to think and to pray before I talk, text, or tweet. Help me to avoid judging others. Help me to avoid "piling on" and kicking someone who is already down.

Yes, sometimes I have to speak hard truths, but let me speak the truth in love, as your Word teaches. Let me speak love and peace and encouragement into others' lives whenever I can. I want to lead by example.

> The mouths of the righteous utter wisdom,
> and their tongues speak what is just.
>
> **PSALM 37:30**

THINK ABOUT IT

A NEW CHAPTER

––––––––

As I begin a new chapter of my life, help me never to be afraid of knowledge. I know that you are the author of truth, so there is no need for me to fear truth. Help me to truly listen to others. Help me to be respectful. As your Word says, help me to be eager to listen but slow to speak and slow to become angry. (I have learned that anger and defensiveness tend to walk hand in hand.)

I should seek first to understand and then to be understood. I don't have to agree with someone to learn from him or her. Remind me that if I want people to respect my perspective, I must do the same for them.

The desire of the righteous ends only in good.

PROVERBS 11:23

Yearning and Learning

If my education has taught me anything, it's that I still have tons to learn. There have been a few things I thought I had mastered. But as I dug deeper, I realized that my perspective was limited. Now I am understanding that I can always benefit from more guidance, insight, patience, and understanding.

Let me look to you as my ultimate source of truth and hope. I don't want to become overly confident in my own understanding. Remind me that I need you. Remind me that true wisdom walks hand in hand with humility. Amen.

> Trust in the Lord with all your heart
> and lean not on your own understanding.
>
> **PROVERBS 3:5**

Actions Follow Attitude

Proverbs 23:7 is an awesome verse: "As [a man] thinks in his heart, so is he" (NKJV). This means that the attitude I choose, toward both God and other people, will set the course for my life.

If I am thankful, humble, and generous, my life is going to go one way. If I am negative, jealous, judgmental, and arrogant, I'll head in a quite different direction. So I pray that my mind will be a positive control center for my life. Let me think good thoughts, pure and true thoughts. Please protect me from any attitudes that will drag me down—along with anyone around me.

When I fall into a pattern of negative thinking, help me to change course. Fill my head and my heart with your goodness.

Finally, brothers and sisters, whatever is true, whatever is noble, whatever is right, whatever is pure, whatever is lovely, whatever is admirable—if anything is excellent or praiseworthy—think about such things.

PHILIPPIANS 4:8

WEAVING WITH TRUTH

———

Dear all-knowing heavenly Father, I praise you and thank you for new opportunities to learn and grow. This is an exciting time to be alive! Please open my eyes and my mind to new truths and insights. I want to be a lifelong learner. I thank you for what I have learned and experienced so far in my life. I want to keep seeking and applying the knowledge that will help me be the best person I can be.

At the same time, I ask you to balance my curiosity with wisdom and contemplation. Be with me as I explore new horizons. May I always weave more and more of your truth into my life. Amen.

The earth and every good thing in it belongs
to the Lord and is yours to enjoy.

1 CORINTHIANS 10:26 TLB

HOLY HUMILITY

A NEW LIGHT

I don't want to sound like a shallow person, but as a new grad, I'll be meeting a lot of new people. This makes me worried about my appearance. The clothes I wear. The way I carry myself. How I look.

Please remind me that you focus on my heart. I am your unique creation. You love and accept me wholeheartedly. With this in mind, I pray that I will not fall into the trap of equating my worth with how I dress or how my hair is behaving (or misbehaving) on any given day.

Thank you for seeing all your children in a different light. Please replace my self-consciousness with others-consciousness. Help me to show grace and love to others. Help me to share in your acceptance of them. Help me to value them as you do.

> God does not see the same way people
> see. People look at the outside of a person,
> but the LORD looks at the heart.
>
> **1 SAMUEL 16:7 NCV**

Humble Heart, Open Mind

———

Having just graduated, I feel good about all I have learned. But sometimes I feel a little too good. I am tempted to think that I know more than I really do. That I can do just fine without a lot of outside advice or assistance.

But from the class president to the class clown, we all have more to learn. I know I need to learn some things for myself, from experience, from trial and error.

However, I need a humble heart and an open mind when it comes to learning from others. It's wise for me to consider what others think and what they have learned from their real-life experiences. There is value in time-tested advice. Just like the advice I find in your Word.

The humble will see their God at work and be glad.

PSALM 69:32 NLT

An Agent of Love

I don't think of myself as a judgmental person, but I am finding it hard to love this one person—well, maybe a couple of people—or even to be civil to them.

When I find myself feeling this way, I know I need you to change my heart. I want to love everyone the way you do… with a good heart and not a drop of prejudice or judgment. I want to love no matter what. And I want to be courageous enough to show that I care. I don't want to be held back by public opinion.

I don't know how else to say it: Help me get over myself. Help me overcome my ego.

I want to be an instrument of your love, not an instrument of pride or prejudice.

> Be kind to one another, tenderhearted, forgiving
> one another, as God in Christ forgave you.
>
> **EPHESIANS 4:32 RSV**

Warning Labels

Being a person of faith can be a challenge. With all the animosity out there, I wonder if people should come with warning labels.

Let me live out my faith in a way that draws people to you and never sends them running away as fast as they can go. Help me to avoid arguments that create barriers and animosity. Help me to love and forgive. Help me build people up, especially when others are trying to tear them down. Help me to be humble, to be a peacemaker. I know people can debate theology and social issues for hours and hours, but those debates have no winners.

I know that our world is always changing and that it includes lots of things to argue about. But who can argue with a life lived Jesus' way? That's the kind of life I want to live.

> Make the most of every opportunity
> you have for doing good.
>
> **EPHESIANS 5:16 TLB**

A Critical Matter

Thank you for accepting me as I am, flaws and all. You have set a perfect standard for me to follow. I want to show this kind of acceptance to my friends and family members. I don't ever want them to wonder if I care about them. I want them to feel valued.

Help me to avoid being overly critical. I don't want to hold back my acceptance. I have found that when I criticize others, it's usually because I am not feeling good about myself. I am focusing on my flaws and dragging others down as a result.

Let me find rest and peace of mind in your grace and love. I know that when I do this, my life will overflow with words and actions that encourage the people in my life. Amen.

Love one another with brotherly affection.
Outdo one another in showing honor.

ROMANS 12:10 ESV

THE BLESSING
OF CONTENTMENT

A Dangerous Word

————

Compare. It's a seemingly innocent word, but it can be a dangerous one. At this point in my life, it's easy to fall into the trap of comparing GPAs, starting salaries, or friends and followers on social media. Then, depending on how I stack up on a given day, I end up feeling prideful…or depressed and discouraged.

Please remind me that my true value is not determined by social media fame, income brackets, rating systems, or any other label people may try to stick on me. I have inherent value because I am your child. You love me. You value me. Help me to remember this ultimate truth. I am at my best when I live my life according to this truth, a truth that sets me free to be the best I can be.

The Lord will guide you always;
he will satisfy your needs.

ISAIAH 58:11

Forgotten Blessings

———

I need to apologize to you right now. I'm sorry for not appreciating all that you have given to me. I tend to focus on what I don't have rather than how much I do have. When I think about things honestly, I realize I have been blessed in a lot of ways.

So I thank you for the abilities you've given me, for the dreams you are growing in my heart. I'm sorry I haven't always put my skills to good use. In some cases, I have flat-out neglected good gifts from your hand.

I want to make the most of what you have given me. I want to use what I have to serve you. I want to do something good for my world. Help me to use what I have. Help me discover my potential and live a life that counts.

> Each of you should use whatever gift you
> have received to serve others, as faithful
> stewards of God's grace in its various forms.
>
> **1 PETER 4:10**

When Ordinary
Becomes Extraordinary

————

M y heavenly Father, I like my life. On some days, I even love my life.

But I don't love all my daily tasks and responsibilities. And being a graduate has heaped even more of this kind of stuff on my plate.

Some tasks are boring. And let's face it—some are… unpleasant. (And that's a kind way of putting it.) But I can do every task with dedication, gratitude, and sometimes even love. What a concept!

I know that when I strive to be present in the everyday moments, I find that you are present too. You are right by my side, even when I'm filling out an endless form or dealing with a pile of laundry I've been ignoring. Your presence makes all the difference. You show me the satisfaction of simply getting stuff done—even the tedious stuff. You can transform the ordinary into the extraordinary.

Humble yourselves, therefore, under God's mighty hand, that he may lift you up in due time. Cast all your anxiety on him because he cares for you.

1 PETER 5:6-7

Patience Pleases God

Lord, you have been so patient with me. I need to ask your forgiveness for the times I have been less patient with others. Your Word is full of examples of how I should live my life, and that includes my private life and my interactions with others.

I realize that my love and kindness toward other people glorifies you. It warms your heart, and it points people toward you. Others will know I am yours when I show the love of Christ to everyone I encounter.

Better a patient person than a warrior,
one with self-control than one who takes a city.

PROVERBS 16:32

WORKING TOGETHER

TOGETHER IS BETTER

D ear God, being part of a team, group, or club is a privilege and a responsibility. Now that I find myself being part of a new group, may I do all I can to make sure we build on a foundation of love, trust, respect, and excellence. May we all work together to be the best we can be. May we show grace to everyone, both within and beyond our group. I hope the people around me will come to realize they can depend on me.

Thank you for watching over us. Please keep us safe and guard us from any kind of harm. And whether we succeed or fail on any given day, may your love triumph over all.

> The LORD is good to those whose hope is in him,
> to the one who seeks him;
> it is good to wait quietly
> for the salvation of the LORD.

LAMENTATIONS 3:25-26

Divinely Placed People

Lord, I am so grateful for the people you have divinely placed in my life. I am blessed to have influencers who speak words of love, truth, and wisdom to me. More importantly, these people *live* these qualities and don't simply talk about them.

Please keep my heart open when caring people are striving to help me, instruct me, and yes, even warn me about the minefield that life can be. Give me the strength and courage to accept sound advice and then to put it into practice.

Above all, fill me with peace. I know that I will miss the mark sometimes, but it comforts me to know that I have caring family and friends who will help me overcome my mistakes. These people are like angels on earth for me, and I will always be thankful for them. Amen.

Two are better than one,
because they have a good return for their labor:
If either of them falls down,
one can help the other up...
A cord of three strands is not quickly broken.

ECCLESIASTES 4:9-10,12

Family Matters

It's a privilege be part of something bigger than myself. I draw strength and comfort from being your child.

I know that in a family, everyone has responsibilities. I enjoy some of these; others, not so much. But I want to serve you. I want to be a family member who contributes something.

Help me see opportunities to serve, to help my brothers and sisters in Christ. Help me to accept responsibilities I have been trying to avoid.

I want to put my whole heart and soul into serving you. I want to set an example that others can follow.

Whoever who does not love does not
know God, because God is love.

1 JOHN 4:8

Relationship Realities

―――――

Even the best people have their bad moments. (I know I do!) Every friendship and every romantic relationship is, at times, a perfect storm of flaws, brokenness, and pain. Help me to be a good friend. Help me to be patient with others' flaws, just as I pray they will be patient with mine.

Give me the courage to look pain and anger in the eye and deal with it rather than running away. Help me refuse to abandon people just because relationships are difficult. Let's face it—all relationships are difficult sometimes.

I will listen to what God the Lord says;
he promises peace to his people, his faithful servants.

PSALM 85:8

A Prayer for Unity

Heavenly Father, who makes us one, may we be your children who encourage each other, listen to each other, learn from each other, speak the truth to each other, forgive each other, and love each other.

Today may I choose my words with care. Today may I lift the spirits of any who struggle. Today may I be willing to forgive and to seek forgiveness. Today may I love others as you have loved me.

In Jesus' name, amen.

Teach me to do your will,
for you are my God;
may your good Spirit
lead me on level ground.

PSALM 143:10

MY SUPPORT SYSTEM

D ear Lord, this new chapter in my life has profoundly affected my support system. Specifically, I don't have all the same friends around me, and I really miss them. Please bring some new friends into my life.

Open my eyes to see the many good qualities in the people around me. At the same time, may people see me in my best light. Help me be the kind of friend people value. I love it when I can encourage my friends, as they do the same for me. I love to spend time with people who are kind, humble, gracious, and wise. The people who reflect Jesus wherever they go, whatever they do.

I pray that my friends, both old and new, will be influenced for good as they spend time with me.

Accept one another, then, just as Christ accepted you.

ROMANS 15:7

TRUE HAPPINESS

Transformed!

———

I n this new chapter of my life, I pray that I will pursue the right things, the best things. I don't want to be defined by my degree, my job title, or my starting salary. Please protect me from even a hint of greed.

There is nothing wrong with success, of course. But life should not be defined by what I have, even if I end up having a lot. I am your child, your follower—that's who I want to be at the core of my life. That is what should inspire me and set the direction of my heart.

> Don't copy the behavior and customs of this world, but
> let God transform you into a new person by changing
> the way you think. Then you will learn to know God's
> will for you, which is good and pleasing and perfect.

ROMANS 12:2 NLT

Life Envy

I must admit it—sometimes I have a case of life envy. Social media is full of people whose lives (and food) seem to be extraordinary all the time. Meanwhile, my life seems rather common. I'm not spending my days parachuting out of airplanes or eating meals that look like works of art.

Help me to understand that "common" does not mean boring or unremarkable. I know that you provide amazing blessings for those with eyes to see them and hearts to appreciate them. A kind word from one of my friends. A simple but delicious meal at my favorite diner. The comfort of crawling into a welcoming bed after a tiring day.

With my eyes set on you and my heart set on thankfulness, my so-called common life can be uncommonly good. I thank you for that.

Be very careful, then, how you live—not as unwise but as wise, making the most of every opportunity.

EPHESIANS 5:15

Possessions in Perspective

Generous God, sometimes I wonder if my possessions own me rather than the other way around. I need your help to live a more generous life. I want my hands to be open to give and serve rather than being clenched around money, a credit card, or the latest tech wonder.

I am grateful for the things I have been able to earn as well as the gifts others have given me. But my stuff is just that—stuff. It's not what life is really all about, and I'm not taking any of it with me when I leave this earth.

Help me keep all my material possessions in their proper place. I want my life to be about so much more than that. Please set my heart on what's eternal, not what's temporary.

Seek first his kingdom and his righteousness, and
all these things will be given to you as well.

MATTHEW 6:33

A Time for Hopes and Dreams

Graduation is a time of hopes and dreams. It's a time to map out a future. It's a time for optimism…but sometimes that optimism can get out of hand. I want to be hopeful and yet realistic about my future. I will not get everything I want. You might not lead me on a path toward piles of money. I probably won't become the next big thing on the internet. However, I know you always fulfill your promises to your people. You will lead me to something better along the road that leads to you. I thank you for that!

I ask for your guidance, especially in times of great confusion and uncertainty. I don't want my ambition to get in the way of your plan for my life. Protect me from pride and anxiety. Keep me grounded in you and your Word. I want to rely on you above anyone or anything else. Most of all, may whatever you have planned for my future bring you glory.

Dear friend, I pray that you may enjoy good
health and that all may go well with you,
even as your soul is getting along well.

3 JOHN 2